To my favorite neighbors ever! I love you! ♡

Megan Kurup

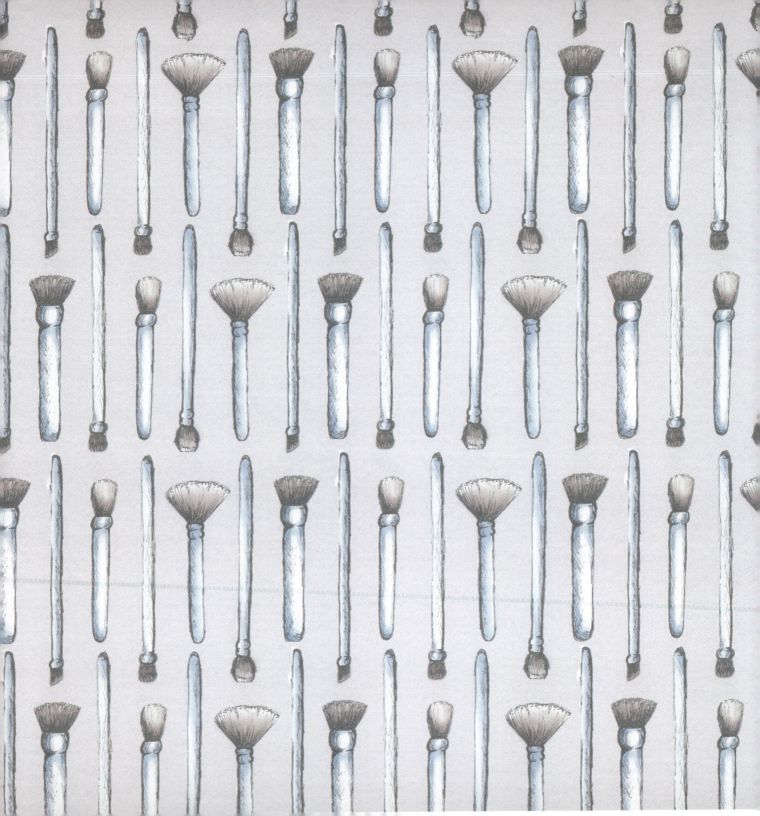

MY MAKEUP MANUAL

A Guide Through the Chaos of Cosmetics

Written and Illustrated by:
Megan E. Keegan

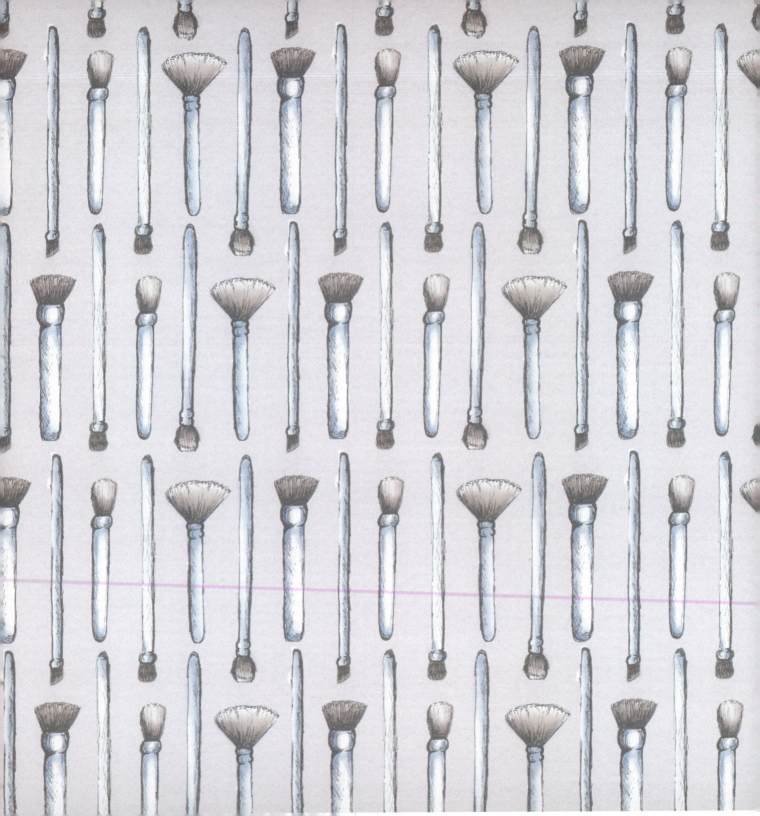

Copyright © 2016 by Megan E. Keegan

All rights reserved. No part of this publication may be reproduced, distributed, or transmitted in any form or by any means, electronic or mechanical, including photocopying, recording, or by any information storage and retrieval system, without the prior permission in writing from to the publisher, except in the case of brief quotations embodied in critical reviews and certain other noncommercial uses permitted by copyright law.

Requests for permission to make copies if any part of the work should be sent to Megan E. Keegan at:
megankeegan317@gmail.com.

Book layout, cover art and design created and copyrighted © 2016 by Megan E. Keegan.

First Printing: 2016

ISBN: 978-1-365-13169-1

Megan Keegan Publishing Co.
Webster Univeristy
St. Louis, MO 63123

Printed in the United States of America.

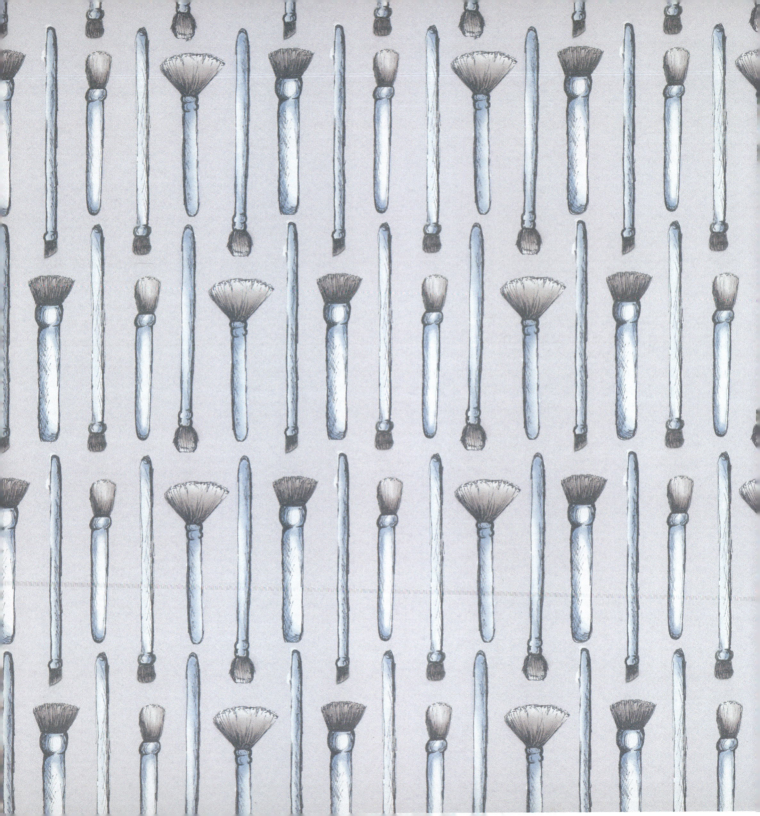

Table of Contents

Introduction 2

Section One - Brushology 4
    Face Brushes 5-6
    Lip & Eye Brushes 7-8

Section Two - Know Your Product 10
    Foundations & You 11-12
    Blushes & Bronzers 13-14
    Wands & Wings 15-16

Section Three - How To's 18
    Contour 19-20
    Smokey Eye 21-22
    Winged Liner 23
    Ombre Lip 24

Section Four - DIY's & Fix Its 26
    DIY: Face Mask 27
    Fix It: Dry Mascara 28
    DIY: Facial Toner 29
    Fix It: Broken Lipstick 30
    DIY: Brush Cleaner 31
    Fix It: Broken Powder 32

Section Five - Swatch Pages 34

Dedication 44

Hey There Gorgeous,

    Unlike celebrities, we do not have a full beauty and makeup team at our dispense every morning while we are getting ready for our day or before we head out for the night. We try to follow tutorials online with makeup gurus who sit in sparkly and brightly lit rooms behind a camera lens, using six different eye shadow palettes that add up to a cost higher than your rent. We try those high-end, fancy-pants makeup stores only to leave either broke buying two items or just even more confused with what products we actually need to conquer these makeup looks. Well girl, you are not alone. We are not professionals. We are ladies who just want an easy guide on how to do our own killer, gorgeous makeup looks, learn about what products we actually need, and master the mayhem that is makeup. This is My Makeup Manual. Inside, you can figure out what you, yourself, actually need without people pushing products in your face. You can also learn from some tools and product knowledge, basic tutorials, and DIY's all in this convenient little beacon of answers.

So crack this bad boy open and let's get started.

SECTION ONE
Brushology

OK girl, before you dive into any makeup-look-mastering, we need to make sure you have the proper tools. Or maybe you just need to clarify what the heck this brush is and what it is used for. I can help with that. While all the variations of brushes can get confusing, here is a breakdown of the basics. See which ones you think you might need.

Face Brushes

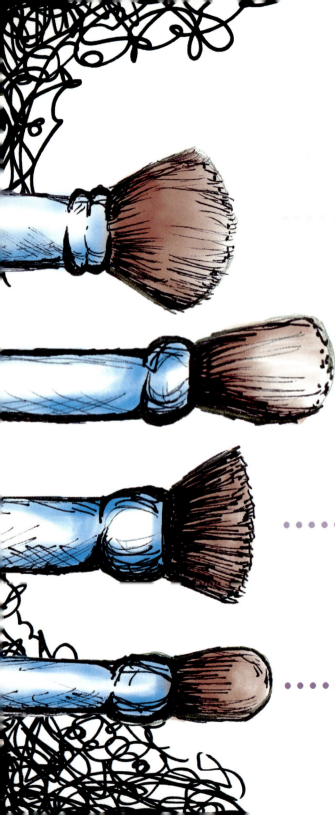

POWDER

Rounded, loosely packed bristles that are typically more fluffy and soft. Best used for loose and pressed powders.

BLUSH

Similar to a powder brush, but just more compacted bristles. Perfect for applying blush on the apples of your cheeks.

STIPPLING

Rounded, densely packed bristles with a flat top. Perfect to apply foundation for a sheer finish or light pigmentation.

TAPERED

Densely packed, flat, flexible bristles. Perfect for the use of applying and blending liquid and cream foundations.

FAN

Soft, loosely packed, flat, fan shaped bristles perfect for gently sweeping on highlighter or light bronzer.

ANGLED

Can be loose or densely packed bristles. Looser and softer bristles are best for applying highlighters, blushes, and bronzers. Denser compacted versions are ideal for a more precise contour.

CONCEALER

Medium sized, flat bristles with rounded, pointed tip. Best use for applying concealers and blending into contours of face.

SPONGE

Comes in a multitude of shapes and sizes. Ideal for applying and blending liquid foundation, spot treatment with concealers, building up foundation coverage.

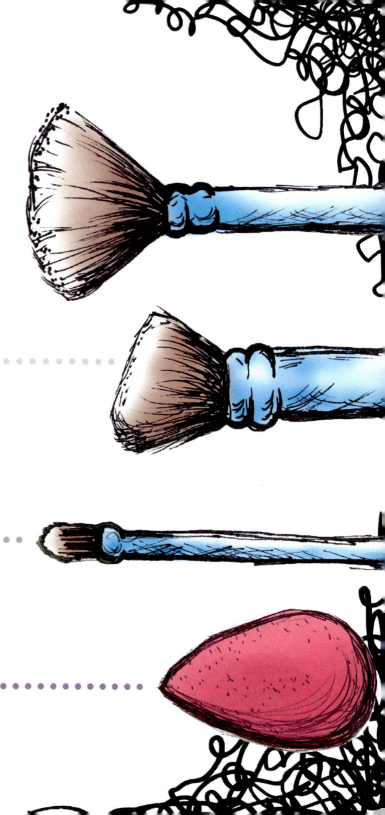

Lip & Eye Brushes

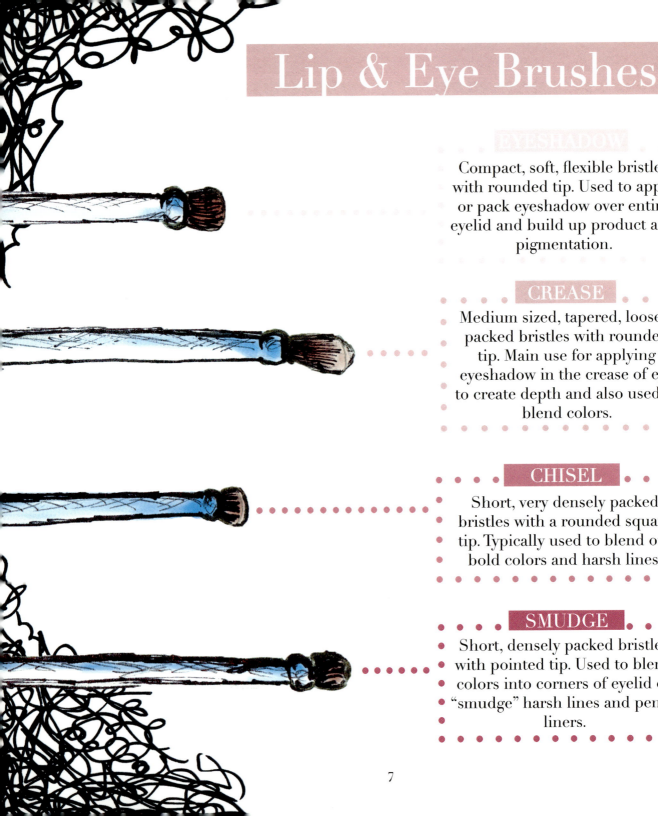

EYESHADOW
Compact, soft, flexible bristles with rounded tip. Used to apply or pack eyeshadow over entire eyelid and build up product and pigmentation.

CREASE
Medium sized, tapered, loosely packed bristles with rounded tip. Main use for applying eyeshadow in the crease of eye to create depth and also used to blend colors.

CHISEL
Short, very densely packed bristles with a rounded square tip. Typically used to blend out bold colors and harsh lines.

SMUDGE
Short, densely packed bristles with pointed tip. Used to blend colors into corners of eyelid or "smudge" harsh lines and pencil liners.

Loosely packed, soft bristles. Miniature version of powder brush. Ideal for a light application of eyeshadows. Also used for blending eyeshadows.

Flat, densely packed, flexible bristles with angled tip. Used to apply cream eyeliners and filling in sparse sections of eyebrows.

LIP

Small, flat, compacted bristles with a rounded tip. Used to apply lipsticks and lip liners with more precision.

MASCARA

Also called a "spoolie" brush, used for either applying liquid mascara, combing eyelashes, and shaping and combing eyebrows.

LINER

Thin, short, flexible compacted bristles. Ideal for applying eyeliner.

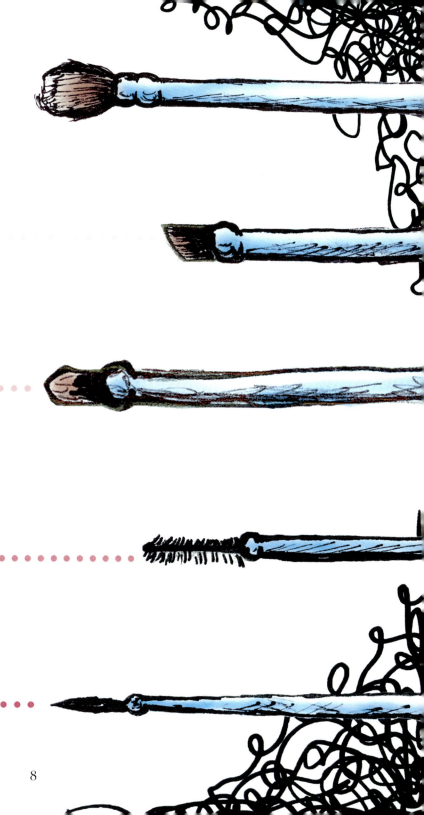

SECTION TWO
Know Your Product

Now let's make sure you are using the best product meant for you. Depending on your skin type and tone, that makeup look can either turn into fabulous or failure if you don't use the correct product or shade that is perfect for you. Let's see you what you need, gorgeous.

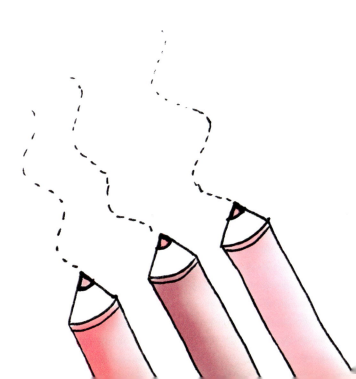

Foundations & You

It is the base of every makeup look: foundation. As with any beauty essential, there are so many options for us girls to choose from that it can leave us feeling lost in finding our perfect fit. To help you through this cosmetic chaos, here is advice on how to pick the best foundation for your skin type.

NORMAL

With normal skin, you are one of the lucky ones. The decision between powders and liquids is really up to you and your personal preference on which textures you like best. So easy!

OILY

If you have oily skin, it can be so annoying to find foundation that looks good all day. To get the shine-free look, it is all in the product formulas you use. With oily skin, you will want to use moisturizers that are water-based and then use foundations that are either powder foundations or liquid foundations that are powder-based. The water based moisturizer will be light enough that it won't clog pores. Powder and powder-based liquid foundations will absorb the oil to give you that matte look. When applying, use a sponge or brush because using your fingers can spread dirt and oil from your hands to your face.

ACNE PRONE

The challenge with acne prone skin is that you have to be careful that the foundation you are using doesn't make matters worse.

With acne prone skin, the oils in products can be the instigator behind those pimples. Look for primers or moisturizers that are labeled as "oil-free". You should also look for foundations with ingredients such as salicylic acid.

This will not only hide those pesky pimples, but also help to prevent any more from coming back. Apply with a clean brush for every application.

DRY

Dry skin can be a temporary problem or a constant problem. Having dry skin when applying foundation can just magnify the trouble dry spots. The key here is to moisturize, moisturize, moisturize. Apply a facial moisturizer before applying your foundation. Then once it is dry, apply a creamy, hydrating foundation to lock it all in using your fingers instead of a brush to really push the product into your skin.

Blushes & Bronzers

When it comes to finding your perfect shade in blushes and bronzers, the rule of thumb is that blushes and bronzers are intended to look natural and enhance your already gorgeous skin tone. Applying the right hue can create that perfectly flushed and sun-kissed bronzed looked. There is a whole spectrum of skin tone shades and an even bigger spectrum of blush and bronzer colors. To make it simple, here is a breakdown. See which one you think you might fall under.

Fair

With blushes, the fair skin toned beauty needs to keep it to a family of soft pinks, peaches, or light corals. These colors will create the perfect accent. When it comes to bronzers, like blushes, find sheer or light bronzers with peach undertones.

Medium

With blushes, for the medium skin tone gal, peaches and pinks will be your best friend. Unlike fair skin tones, you will need to step towards deeper and richer shades of the peach and pink family. In bronzers, you will look amazing in soft shades of copper and earthy browns.

Dark

With blushes, you dark skin tone darlings will want to accent your skin tone with deep shades of red, orange, fuchsia, and brown. These rich shades will give you radiance to match your gorgeous skin. Pair your skin tone and blush with bronzers that are rich chocolate browns or ones of shimmery hues and formulas to give you that glowing appearance.

Wands & Wings

It may seem like they don't make a difference, but when it comes to the mascara wands and the eyeliner product, it can make all the difference on the look as a whole. Each one is best for something else, see which one you think you can rock.

Round: Defined Lower Lashes

 **Conetaper:** Winged Outer Lashes

Curved: Fanned-Out Lashes

 **Balled Tip:** Detailed Corner Lashes

Micro: Natural Lower Lashes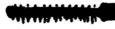

 **Rubber:** Defined Length Lashes

Flat Comb: Separated and Dark Lashes

 **Oversized:** Maximum Volume Lashes

EYELINER TYPES:

POWDER

Use a liner brush or angled liner brush and black or dark eyeshadow colors for a natural and subtle eyeliner look.

PENCIL

Made of a dry and creamy formula, used to make natural liner looks or softer liner lines. Best for lower lash line or inner tight line. Pigmentation is dependent on the weight of application.

GEL

Made of a creamy formula that can smear, use this with a liner brush or angled liner brush to create dark thin or thick liner looks.

LIQUID

Fast drying liquid formulas are used to create dramatic dark liner looks with thin or thick lines and excellent precision.

SECTION THREE
How To's

We are busy ladies. We don't have time to sit around and watch a video tutorial that has countless amount of steps and products. They just over complicate things. What you need is a breakdown of the basics. You need tutorials on common makeup looks that get right into business. You have places to be and that is no reason to sacrifice putting together a killer contour and a sassy smokey eye. So let's simplify these things. In this section, you will find just that. Interpret these looks however you want and cut out any unneeded steps to accommodate your own glamorous style. Now grab your brushes and your palettes and let's get started.

How To: Contour

Step 1: Using either a sponge, powder brush, stippling brush, or tapered foundation brush, apply foundation evenly over entire face and neck.

Step 2: Using an angled brush, locate the hallows of your cheek bones and lightly apply bronzer in a circular diagonal motion angled towards the corner of your mouth.

Step 3: Using the same brush or a powder brush, create a "3" on either side of your face connecting the cheekbone contour to temples of your forehead and lower jaw line.
• Optional: Use a chisel brush or eyeshadow brush to apply bronzer to the sides of nose for an even more sculpted look.

Step 4: Using a clean sponge or concealer brush, apply concealer or a lighter foundation to the negative spaces of the bronzer lines (top of cheekbones, lower cheek, bridge of nose, chin, and forehead).

Step 5: Using a clean sponge or powder brush, blend all product lines together in circular motions.

Step 6: Using fan brush, lightly dust highlight powder to the tops of your cheekbones.

Step 7: Using a blush brush, gently sweep blush from apples of cheek lightly up into highlight and upper cheek bones.

Step 8: Apply setting powder or setting spray to hold all into place for long-lasting wear.

How To: Smokey Eye

Step 1: Prime the eyelid (optional) and then, using eyeshadow brush, cover the eyelid and the brow bone in a neutral or the lightest eyeshadow shade.

Step 2: Using a fluff brush or a clean eyeshadow brush, apply the second to lightest eyeshadow color only on the eyelid area.

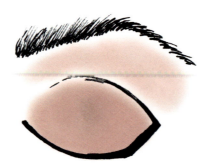

Step 3: Using a crease brush, apply the medium eyeshadow shade to the crease of the eye in soft windshield wiper motions. Be sure to not focus on the eyelid, just the crease above it where the eyelid folds.

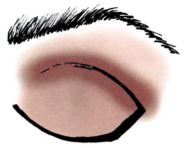

Step 4: Using a clean crease brush or the tip of a clean eyeshadow brush, apply a triangle of the darkest eyeshadow shade to the corner of the eye. Thoroughly blend out using smudge brush or chisel brush.

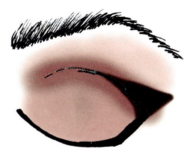

Step 5: Blend out all of the harsh lines and color shade transitions with a clean fluff brush.

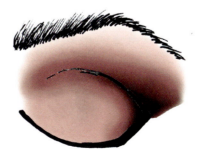

How To: Winged Liner

Step 1: Using an eyeliner or angled liner brush, draw a small fine line from the corner of the eye up towards the end of your eyebrow.

Step 2: Connect a fine, thin line from the tip of the first line back towards eyelid edge. This will determine the thickness of the wing.

Step 3: Fill in the space between the two lines that you created in steps 1 and 2.

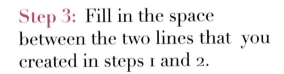

Step 4: Line the rest of the eyelid a far as you prefer with a gradual line to connect the wing and create a smooth, fierce look.

How To: Ombre Lip

Step 1: Find 3 lipstick shades of the same color family in shades that are light, medium and dark.

Step 2: Apply a thin layer of chapstick. Then paint your lips in the medium shade.

Step 3: Using a lip brush, outline your lips with the darkest color. You may also use a darker lip liner instead.

Step 4: Using a clean lip brush, add the lightest shade to the center of the lips for a highlight and focal point.

Step 5: Blend with a clean lip brush or just rub your lips together to mix the colors.

SECTION FOUR
DIY's & Fix Its

We are beauties on a budget. Meaning, we don't have the expense to waste our products or buy name brand beauty essentials on the daily. Good thing there is a way around cashing out your money on almost everything beauty related. So I did you a favor and gathered up some of, what I think, are the most useful hacks you should know. We are friends now, right? Right. So this is my gift to you my B.B.F.L.
(Beauty Bestie For Life).

DIY: Face Mask

■ **Dry Skin Mask:** Mix greek yogurt, avocado, honey and olive oil ■

The fatty acids in this super combo help your skin retain water, drinking up moisture and leaving your skin so soft. Scoop out half of the avocado and mash thoroughly. Mix together with the yogurt, then stir in two tablespoons each of olive oil and honey to create a thick paste. Apply and relax for 20 minutes to let your skin soak up all that needed moisture.
Rinse with warm water.

■ **Acne Prone / Oily Skin Mask:** Mix greek yogurt, lemon, banana, and turmeric ■

This mask stops the growth of blemish-causing bacteria and curbs the oil production in your pores. Mash half of a ripe banana thoroughly and mix with yogurt, half of a squeezed lemon's juice, and then stir in one tablespoon of turmeric powder. Let the mask sit on skin for at least 15 minutes to clear out and refresh all of your pores. Rinse with warm water.

■ **Dull Skin Mask:** Mix Greek yogurt, lemon, honey, and cinnamon ■

This tasty mask frees you of dead cells and boosts circulation to the surface of your skin. Mix one tablespoon each of freshly squeezed lemon juice and honey with the greek yogurt. Add a pinch or two of cinnamon and mix, blending all of the ingredients together. Layer on your face and let sit for 20 minutes. Rinse with warm water.

FIX IT: Dry Mascara

Mascara is one cosmetic product with the shortest lifespan. Normally, any mascara lasts upto three months after opening, if used daily. Because of air entering into the tube and being sealed after use, the air causes the product to dry up and stick.

Here is a solution to restore your dry, clumpy mascara and bring it back to life.

1. Get a bottle of eye drops.

2. Add a few drops into the mascara tube.

3. Stir easily.

Just like that, you got you mascara for at least another month. Long live the lashes.

DIY: Facial Toner

To keep your skin smooth, vibrant, and an even tone - a zesty, fresh facial toner is the way to go. Not only is this toner very refreshing, but it is also easy to make again and again.

YOU WILL NEED:
1/2 Cup of Water
Lemon Half
Tea Tree Oil
1 tsp Sea Salt
2 Mint Leaves
Spray Bottle

First, you need a bottle. You can purchase a small squirt bottle from any craft store. This will be what you can keep your toner in. Either mixing before or adding directly into squirt bottle, mix the water, sea salt, mint leaves, a splash of lemon juice, and 8-10 droplets of tea tree oil.

Mix and shake thoroughly, then refrigerate overnight.

So simple. So refreshing. So beneficial.

FIX IT: Broken Lipstick

To fix this catastrophe, simply take the end of one broken piece and, with a small match or lighter, bring the broken end near the flame until you see visible signs of melting.

Quickly bind both broken ends together as the lipstick dries.

After holding for a minute, take the flame again along the seam of where the two pieces are now bound until there are again visible signs of melting to create the bond.

Wait to dry.

Good as new.

DIY: Brush Cleaner

Brushes get gross. They are not only full of old product, but they are also holding all sorts of oils, bacteria, dust, and dead skin cells. It is important to keep them clean regularly not only for the sake of keeping your skin clear, but it will also make applying makeup with them so much easier. So here is a simple cleaner that will keep your brushes in check:

- One cup of warm water
- A squirt of liquid dish soap
- A splash of vinegar

1. Combine by stirring all ingredients into a jar, glass, or bowl.

2. Take your makeup brush and swirl it into the mixture making sure to rub the bristle against the bottom of the cup.

3. Take out of the mixture and rinse in lukewarm water. Repeat if necessary.

4. To Dry: Place on towel or hang upside down using a towel rack and hair ties.

* If water seeps into the glue of the bristles, the glue will become weak and the bristles will fall out easily.

FIX IT: Broken Powder

It happens to all of us. We are running out the door in a hurry and applying that one last and final touch up — and then it happens. The compact slips out of your hands or gets knocked off the counter and all you hear is the hard crack of the product inside and the even louder crack of your heart. There really should be an emergency room for these tragedies that can happen to your favorite blush. Well, we got the next best thing, sister.

Step 1: Wrap up the compact of broken powder, blush, or eyeshadow in clear plastic wrap. Make sure it adheres tightly to contain everything.

Step 2: Gently crush powder even more turning the pressed powder into a loose powder.

Step 3: Unwrap and add 10 droppers full of rubbing alcohol. You can add a few more droppers full one at a time to see how much you need to get the mixture to a dry, creamy consistency.

Step 4: The powder now is very sponge-like and pliable. Pat and smooth everything back into place with a flat utensil like a butter knife and smooth the powder even further with a flat, dense brush.

SECTION FIVE
Swatch Pages

Now that you have it all down, go out there and conquer that contour with your favorite products. Here you can swatch any of your products or products that you have in mind to purchase to help see which ones you hate, like, love, and just got to have.

SWATCHES

TYPE:
BRAND:
SHADE:
PRICE:
NOTES:

TYPE:
BRAND:
SHADE:
PRICE:
NOTES:

TYPE:
BRAND:
SHADE:
PRICE:
NOTES:

SWATCHES

TYPE:
BRAND:
SHADE:
PRICE:
NOTES:

TYPE:
BRAND:
SHADE:
PRICE:
NOTES:

TYPE:
BRAND:
SHADE:
PRICE:
NOTES:

SWATCHES

TYPE:
BRAND:
SHADE:
PRICE:
NOTES:

TYPE:
BRAND:
SHADE:
PRICE:
NOTES:

TYPE:
BRAND:
SHADE:
PRICE:
NOTES:

SWATCHES

TYPE:
BRAND:
SHADE:
PRICE:
NOTES:

TYPE:
BRAND:
SHADE:
PRICE:
NOTES:

TYPE:
BRAND:
SHADE:
PRICE:
NOTES:

SWATCHES

TYPE:
BRAND:
SHADE:
PRICE:
NOTES:

TYPE:
BRAND:
SHADE:
PRICE:
NOTES:

TYPE:
BRAND:
SHADE:
PRICE:
NOTES:

SWATCHES

TYPE:
BRAND:
SHADE:
PRICE:
NOTES:

TYPE:
BRAND:
SHADE:
PRICE:
NOTES:

TYPE:
BRAND:
SHADE:
PRICE:
NOTES:

SWATCHES

TYPE:
BRAND:
SHADE:
PRICE:
NOTES:

TYPE:
BRAND:
SHADE:
PRICE:
NOTES:

TYPE:
BRAND:
SHADE:
PRICE:
NOTES:

SWATCHES

TYPE:
BRAND:
SHADE:
PRICE:
NOTES:

TYPE:
BRAND:
SHADE:
PRICE:
NOTES:

TYPE:
BRAND:
SHADE:
PRICE:
NOTES:

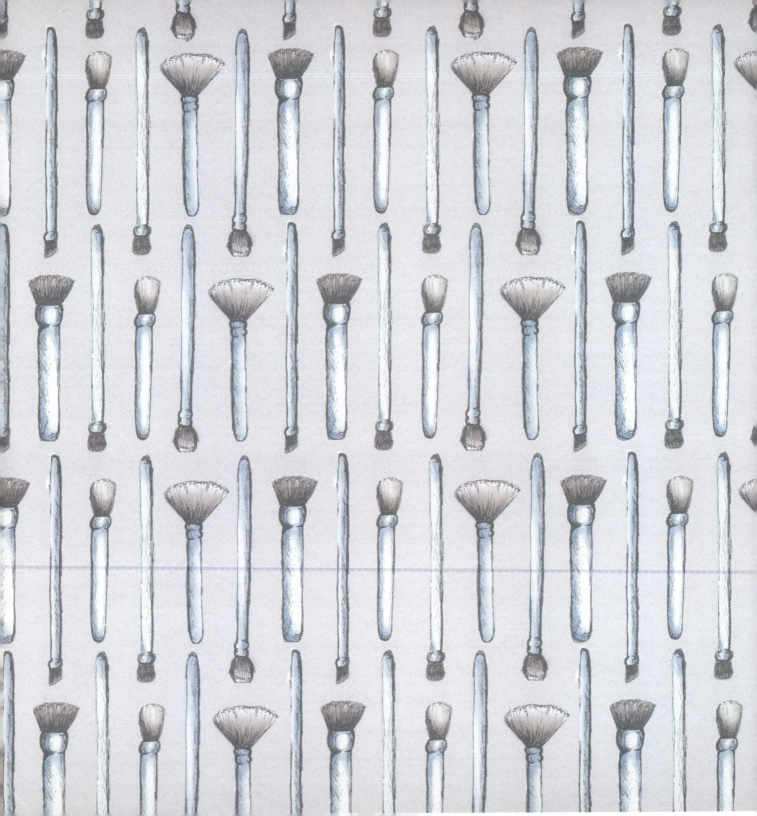

• •

I dedicate this book to all of you beautiful people.

• •